Given to:

_____

From:

_____

On:

_____

"And you must teach My words to your children, talking about them when you are at home,when you go places, when you get ready to sleep, and when you wake up." **Deuteronomy 11:19** (Paraphrased)

But Jesus said, "Let little children be with Me, don't keep them away; because they belong in God's heavenly kingdom." **Matthew 19:14** (Paraphrased)

The Shapes and Colors Bible

Printed in the United States of America
ISBN 0-9741091-3-4
Library of Congress Control Number: 2003093140

Published by The Smart Life Ministries, Inc.
1649 Springhill Street
Chillicothe, MO 64601
www.thesmartlife.org
info@thesmartlife.org

The
Shapes & Colors
Bible

Retold & Illustrated
By
Greg Hughes

Published
By
The Smart Life Ministries
Chillicothe, MO

Contents

Old Testament

New Testament

New Testament

The Old Testament

Genesis

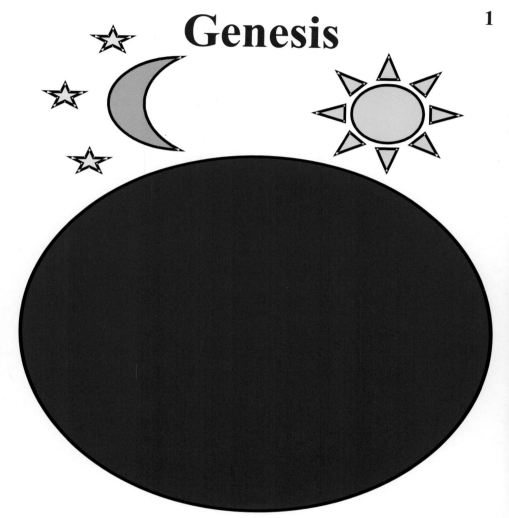

God's Creation

God made the heavens. He created the earth.
He formed it all in six days. Then He rested.

Genesis

The Fall

God made man and woman. But they disobeyed Him.
Then God had Adam and Eve leave His garden.

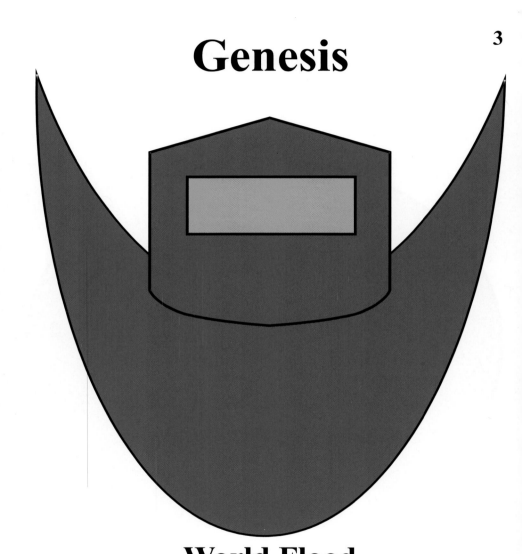

World Flood

Noah built an ark. His family and the animals sailed the waters. God saved them all from the great flood.

Genesis

Abraham Believes

God promised Abraham and Sarah a son. Abraham believed God. Sarah gave birth to their son, Isaac.

Genesis

Israel's Sons

Jacob had twelve sons. His sons sold their brother, Joseph, into slavery. In Egypt, Joseph fed his hungry brothers.

Exodus

Moses Leads

God called Moses. Moses led the Hebrew slaves out of Egypt. Moses taught them about God and His laws.

Leviticus

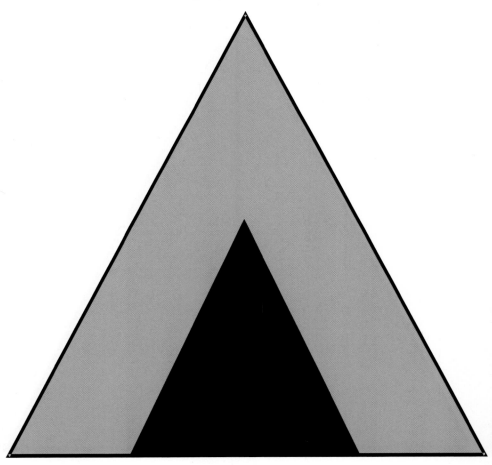

Be Holy

Aaron led worship in God's holy tent. God's people were to be good. He promised to bless Israel's loyalty.

Numbers

Desert Wandering

Israel rejected God's promised land. God sent them into the desert. God's people lived in the wilderness for forty years.

Deuteronomy

I.

II.

III.

IV.

V.

VI.

VII.

VIII.

IX.

X.

God's Laws

Serve no other gods. Have no idols. Honor God's name.
Keep Sabbath rest. Honor mom and dad. Do not kill.
Be faithful. Do not steal. Do not lie. Do not envy.

Joshua

Promised Land

Joshua led Israel. God's people fought to live in Canaan. God made Jericho's walls fall down.

Judges

Heroes Rescue

Wise Deborah saved Israel. Gideon's army defeated Midian. Strong Sampson crushed his enemies.

Ruth

Blessed Trust

Ruth's husband died. She joined his family, nation
and God. Ruth married a farmer, Boaz, and had a son.

1 Samuel

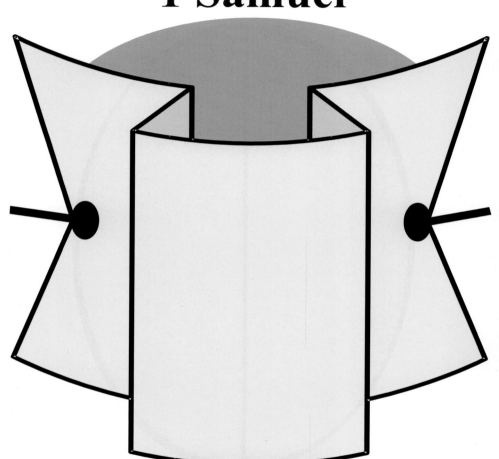

God's Leaders

Hannah's son, Samuel, guided Israel. Saul failed as king. David killed a giant, and later ruled Israel.

2 Samuel

King David

David was a man after God's own heart. He had victories as Israel's king. David also met hard times.

1 Kings

Wayward Kings

Solomon was Israel's wisest and richest king.
The prophet, Elijah, faced bad King Ahab.

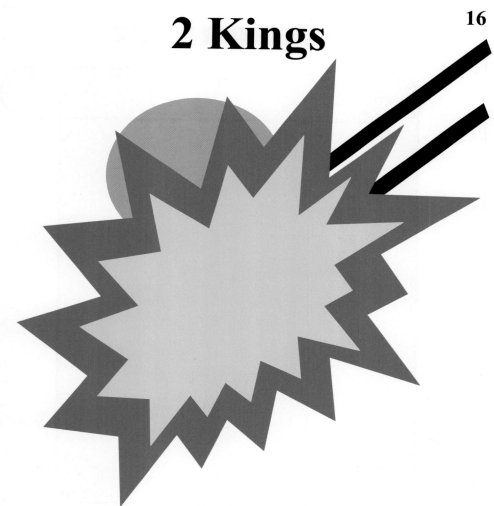

2 Kings

Answered Calls

When Elijah left, Elisha became prophet to Israel.
King Hezekiah turned Judah back to loving God.

1 Chronicles

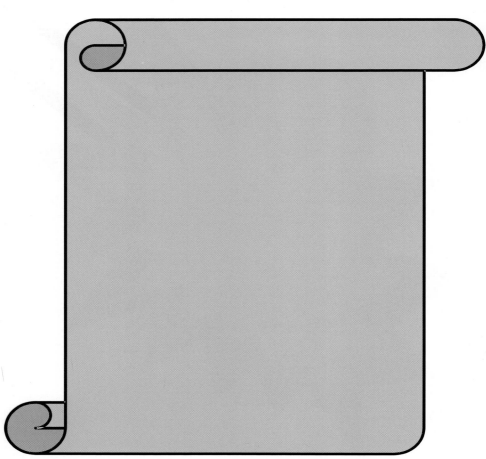

Godly Ways

God's people learned about their family history.
King David helped them worship God.

2 Chronicles

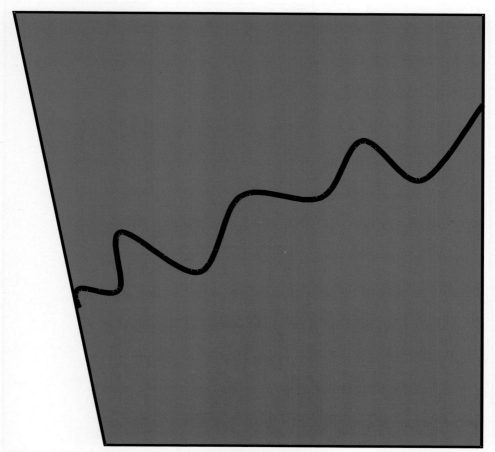

Split Kingdom

Solomon's son, Rehoboam, became king. He treated God's people badly. God's nation divided.

Ezra

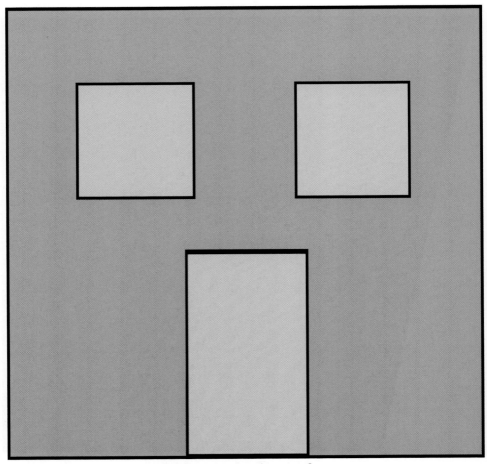

Home Again

King Cyrus helped God's people return home.
God blessed Ezra. He led the Jews in God's ways.

Nehemiah

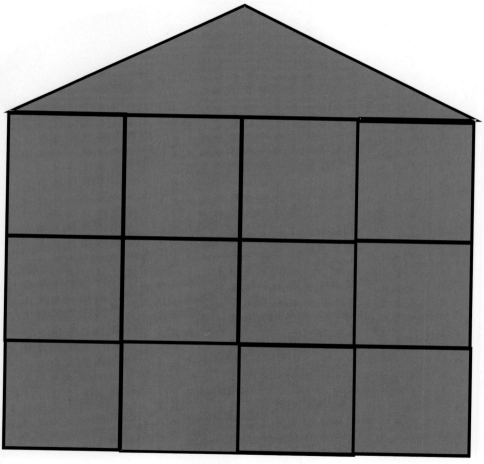

Made New

The city of Jerusalem was a mess. Nehemiah asked God for help. Its citizens and city walls were fixed.

Esther

Called Queen

Esther's cousin was Mordecai. He helped her as
Persia's queen. Esther guarded the Jews from harm.

Job

Hard Times

Job feared God. The devil ruined Job's life. God told Job to trust Him. Then God blessed Job.

Psalms

Praising God

God's people sang praises to Him. They praised the Lord for His greatness, love and friendship.

Proverbs

Wise Path

Wise people seek God's ways. The wise are blessed. Fools disobey God. The wicked suffer.

Ecclesiastes

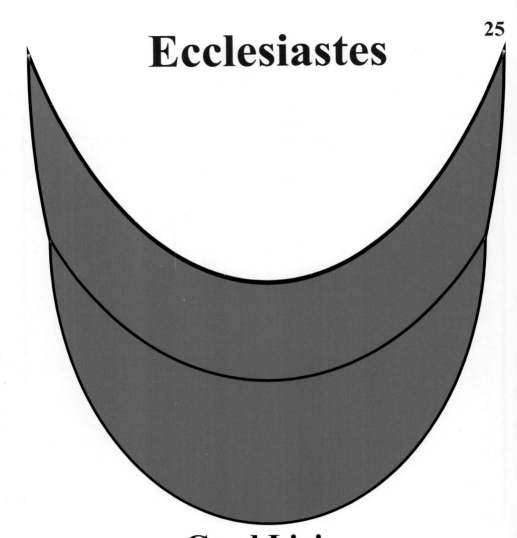

Good Living
Life without God is empty. Nothing can replace Him. True joy comes from knowing the Lord.

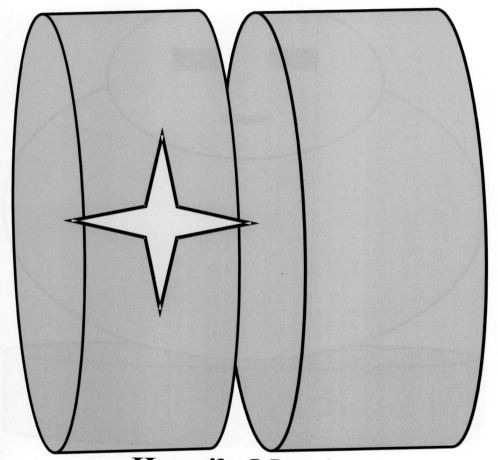

Happily Married

God unites husband and wife. They love God
and each other. God blesses them with His love.

Isaiah

Trust God

God showed Isaiah His holiness. But Judah loved idols. His people needed to trust God and His Savior.

Jeremiah

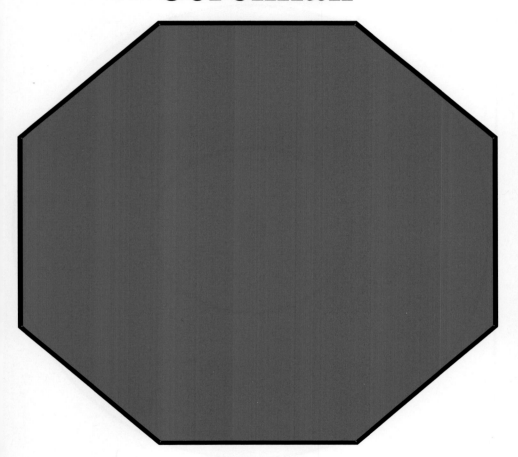

Sinful Nation

God called young Jeremiah. He told the Jews their future troubles. Sinful Judah needed to love God instead.

Lamentations

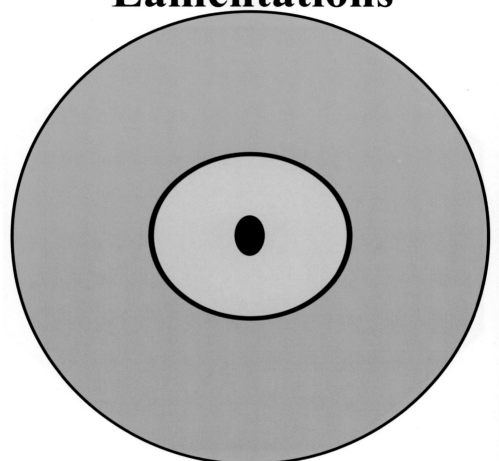

Punished People

Babylon destroyed the nation of Judah. God's people were taken away. But God promised to bless their future.

Ezekiel

Promises Declared

Ezekiel shared with Judah. God would rebuild His nation. The Lord would be with them forever.

Daniel

Standing Firm

Daniel and his friends served God. They lived among enemies. God protected them from harm.

Hosea

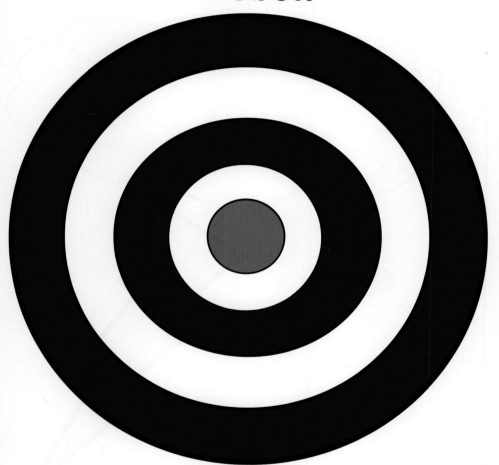

Faithful Love

God promised to heal Israel's heart. Hosea told Israel of God's care. Israel needed to honor God.

Joel

God's Day

God pledged to judge the nations. Joel spoke of God's blessings. God had good things for Judah.

Amos

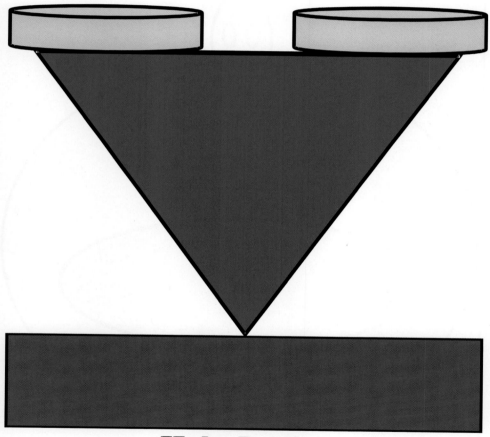

Holy Justice

Israel disobeyed God. The Lord would punish His people. Amos, the shepherd, told them to live for God.

Obadiah

Edom's Trouble

God was upset. Edom bragged about hurting Jacob.
But Israel's tribes would enjoy God's kingdom.

Jonah

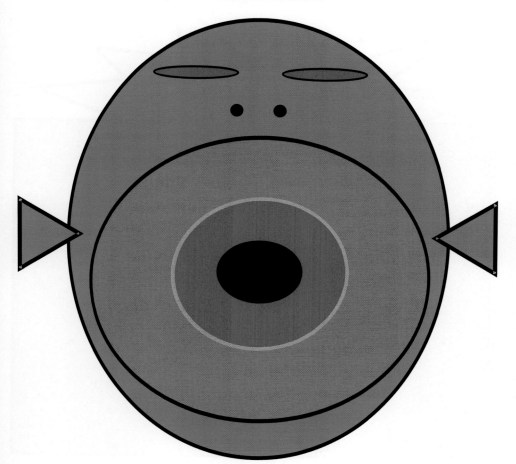

Upset Servant

Jonah sailed away from God. A big fish ate Jonah.
God showed mercy to Jonah and the city of Nineveh.

Micah

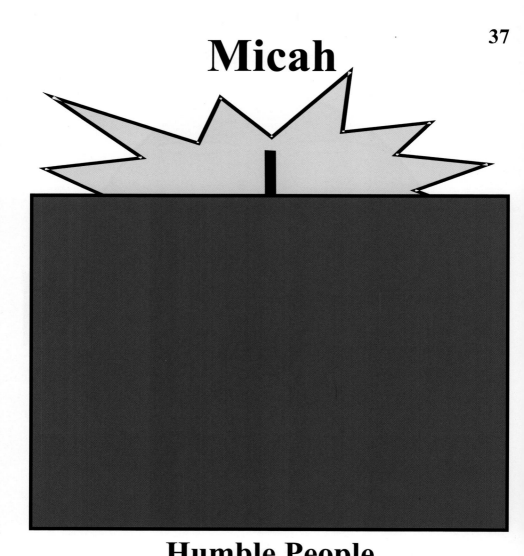

Humble People

God's children acted wrong. He would punish them.
The Lord wanted loyal helpers for His kingdom.

Nahum

Pledged Punishment

Nahum told of God's power. The wickedness of the
city, Nineveh, brought ruin. Nineveh's victims were glad.

Habakkuk

God Wins

God was Habakkuk's strength. God rules over all evil. Habakkuk rejoiced in God's promise of victory.

Zephaniah

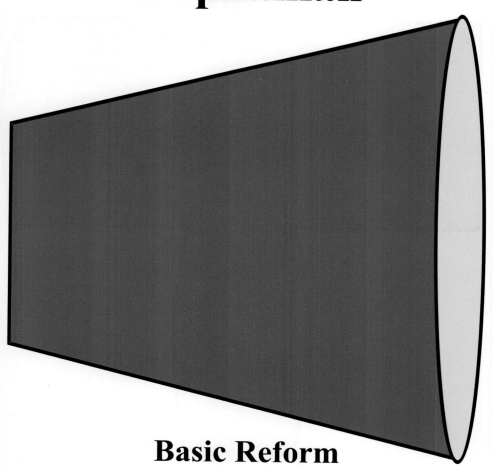

Basic Reform

Zephaniah spoke of God's word. The Lord wanted His people to seek Him. God punished those who left Him.

Haggai

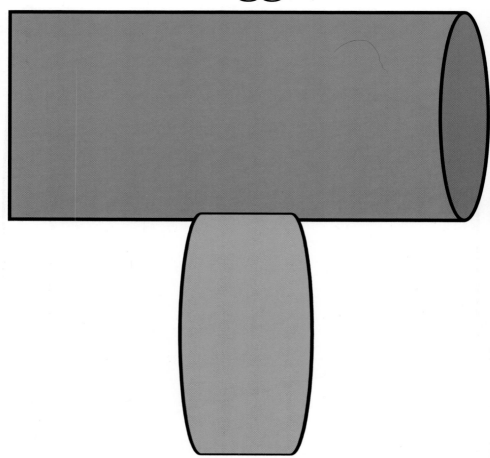

Temple Repairs

God spoke to Haggai. God's people did not care for His temple. The Lord wanted His special place fixed.

Zechariah

Special Plans

Zechariah told God's people to seek Him. God's chosen One would be King of all. He would bring new life to His people.

Malachi

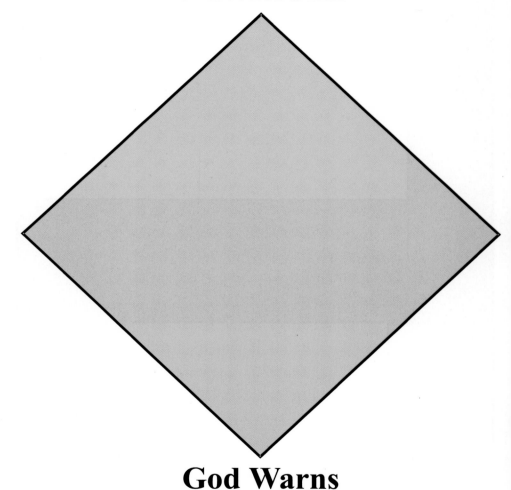

God Warns

Israel worshiped God wrong. Its families were hurt.
People didn't share. They needed to obey the Lord.

The New Testament

Matthew

King Jesus

The Virgin Mary gave birth to Jesus in Bethlehem.
John baptized Jesus. Jesus taught people about God.

Mark

God's Son

Jesus healed many hurting people. He multiplied the fish and loaves. Jesus even calmed the stormy sea.

Luke

The Savior

Jesus gleamed bright on the mountain. He taught His disciples to pray. Jesus helped little Zaccheus find God.

John

Eternal Son

Jesus entered a cheering Jerusalem. He ate His last supper. Jesus died on a cross. But then He rose again.

Acts

Holy Power

Jesus went to heaven. His friends were filled with God's Spirit. Jesus' followers told others about Him.

Romans

Gospel Truth

Paul wrote the Roman Christians. He explained the trouble with sin. Paul shared about God's forgiveness.

1 Corinthians

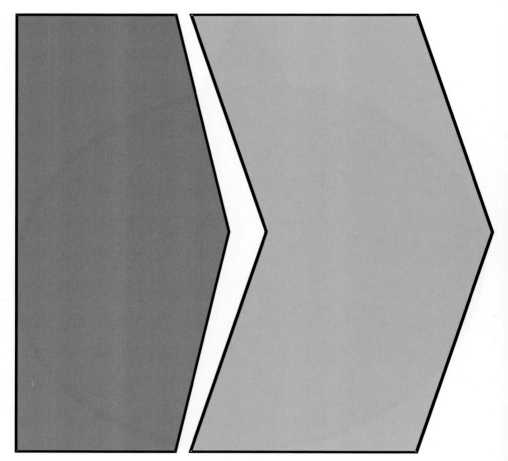

Grow Up

Paul urged the Corinthian church to unite. Christ's love would help them. Jesus' rising again offered them hope.

2 Corinthians

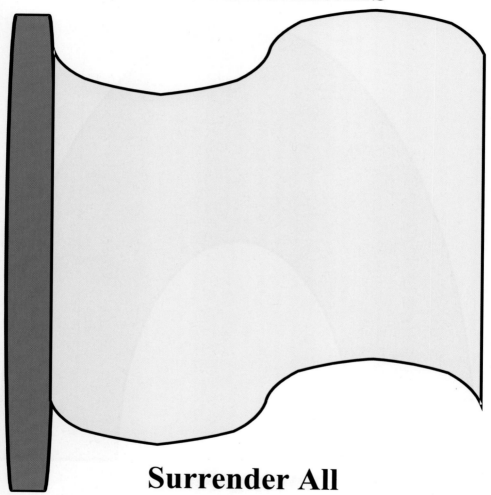

Surrender All

Paul asked the Corinthians for respect. They needed to live for Christ. All Christians must give cheerfully.

Galatians

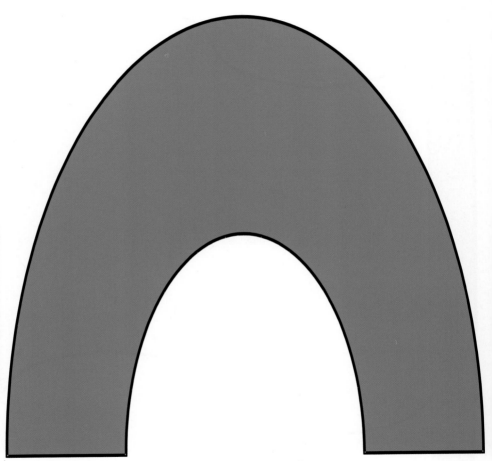

Saving Faith

Paul cared for the Galatians. They learned to trust Jesus for new life. Paul taught them to live by God's Spirit.

Ephesians

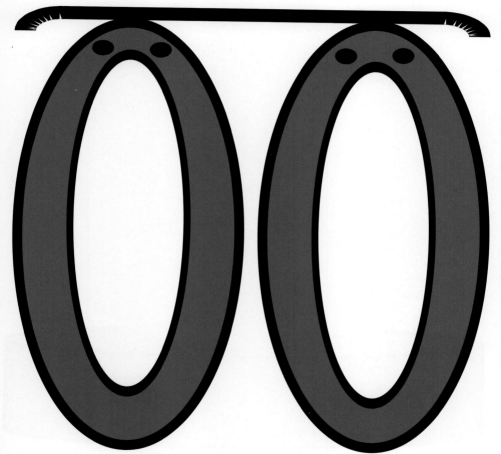

Christian Living

The Ephesians discovered God's forgiveness. They were called to serve God. His Spirit made them strong.

Philippians

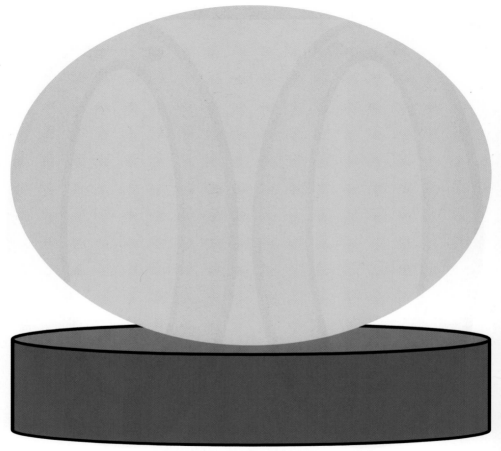

Christ's Victory

Paul told the Philippians of God's work. God praised
His Son, Jesus. Christ can make all Christians champs.

Colossians

Jesus Leads

The Colossians learned about Jesus. Christ rules over everything. Jesus makes believers in Him right with God.

1 Thessalonians

Growth Plan

Paul helped the Thessalonians know Christ. They grew in the faith. Paul taught them about Jesus coming back.

2 Thessalonians

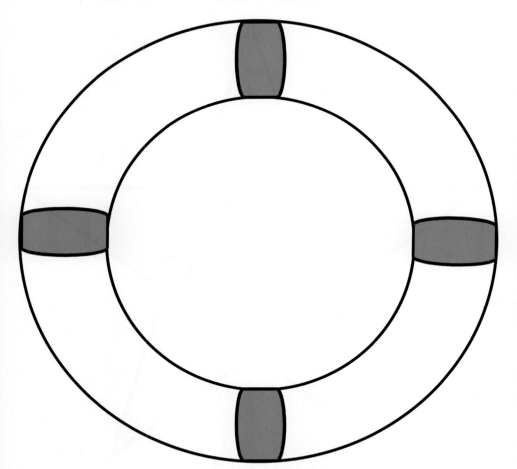

Rescue Mission

Paul told of earth's sad end. But God offered hope.
God's Son would save the Thessalonian Christians.

1 Timothy

Christian Ways

Paul taught Timothy to tell no lies. Timothy believed in God's truth. He learned about Jesus and the church.

2 Timothy

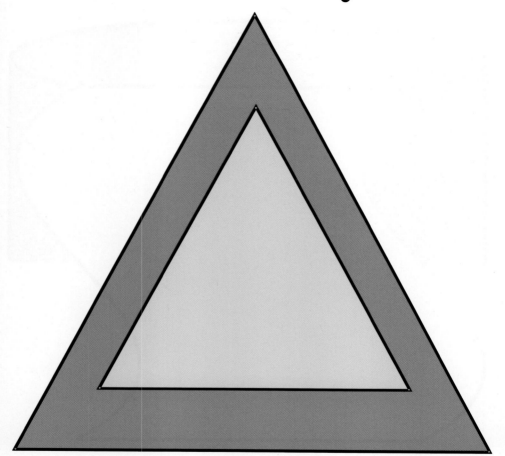

Truthful Lives

Paul coached Timothy about God. He was to guard his faith. Timothy trained others how to live for God.

Titus

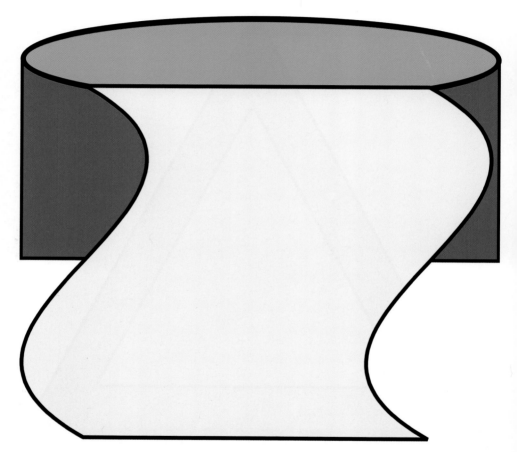

Serving God

Paul trusted Titus to train leaders. Titus taught the Cretian church. They learned about serving God and others.

Philemon

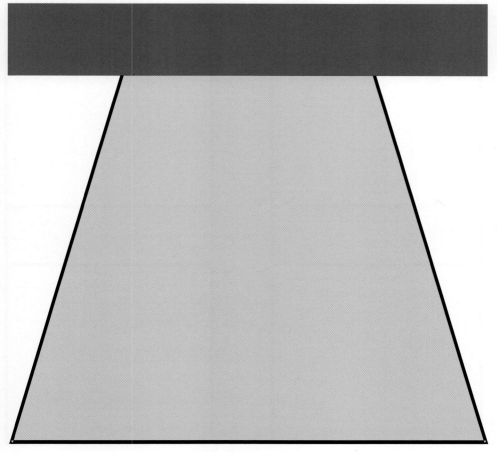

Set Free

Paul wanted Philemon's help. Paul asked him to accept his runaway slave. Onesimus was already free in Christ.

Hebrews

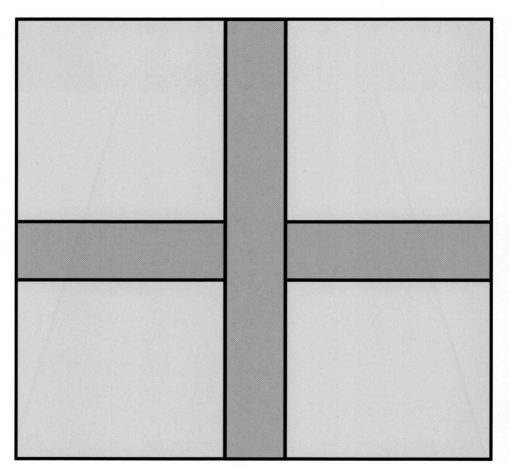

Greatest Gift

God's Son, Jesus, is full of His Father's glory. He died
for our sins. Jesus provides victory for all who trust in Him.

James

Quality Faith

James wrote about God's wisdom. God helps people love each other. People must live out their faith.

1 Peter

Godly Models

Peter shared about a new life in Christ. Christians must obey Jesus. They need to tell others about Him.

2 Peter

Fighting Falsehood

God provides power for holy living. Peter saw God's might in Jesus. God will punish those who reject Him.

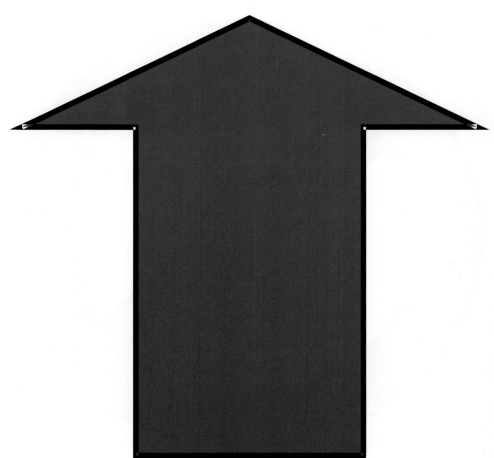

1 John

God's Salvation

John taught that accepting Jesus brings God's forgiveness.
He gives eternal life through Jesus Christ, His Son.

2 John

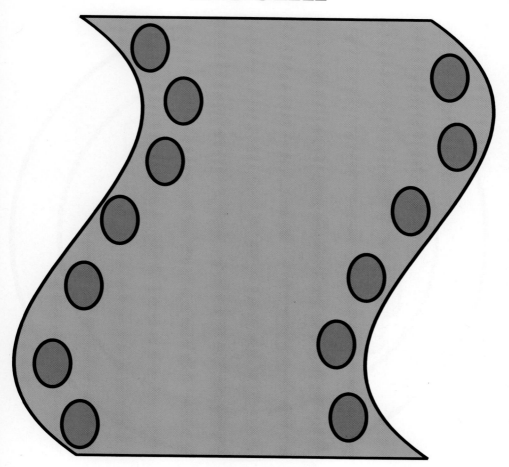

Faith Walk

John asked Christians to love each other. They must follow God's ways. Christians must not lie to others.

3 John

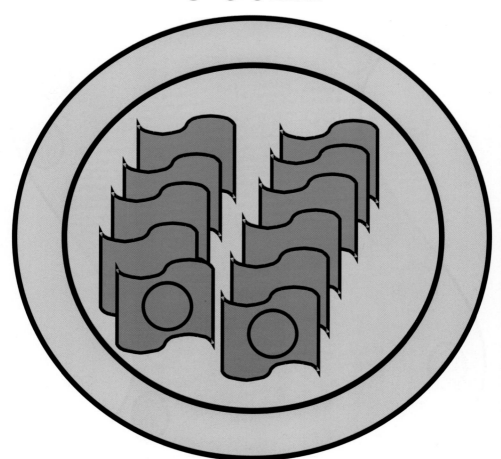

Bless Others

John said living by God's truth is important. Christians must also share. It helps believers bless other people.

Jude

Spiritual Guard

Jude shared about God's protection from false teachers.
God's Spirit helps Christians know His holy word.

Revelation

God Rules

Jesus showed the church His power. God will win over all evil. Jesus will return heaven to earth.

The Shapes & Colors Bible

Kids can learn to trust God and walk with Him through The Shapes & Colors Bible. Shapes, colors and words help teach children basic learning skills. And unlike most children's Bibles, every single book of the Bible is retold through 70 pictures and stories found in The Shapes & Colors Bible. God and His word are waiting for you.

Order Form
The Shapes & Colors Bible

ITEM	QUANTITY	TOTAL
Book: $7.99		
VHS Tape: $7.99		
DVD: $9.99		
	Product Total	
*Shipping	Add 20% to product total	
	Total Amount	

*International rates add 40% of product total

Name   (please print)

Address

City   State   Zip

Please send check or money order payable to:
The Smart Life Ministries
1649 Springhill St., Chillicothe, MO 64601
660-247-2730
info@thesmartlife.org
www.thesmartlife.org

The Mission of The Smart Life Ministries

Empower   **Equip**   **Embrace**

The Smart Life Ministries exists to EMPOWER PEOPLE in EQUIPPING KIDS to EMBRACE JESUS CHRIST.

The Vision of The Smart Life Ministries

The Smart Life Ministries was formed in August of 2002 with the vision of assisting families in instructing their children in the Christian faith. The Shapes and Colors Bible helps teach young children shapes, colors and stories from all 66 books of the Bible. This Bible was designed to help children know God and understand His plan for their lives.

The Smart Life Ministries, a non-profit, 501 (c) (3) interdenominational organization, is dedicated to helping strengthen the ongoing work of local churches, Christian organizations and families in equipping kids to embrace Jesus Christ. The main goal of The Smart Life Ministries is to reach every child in the world with a copy of The Shapes and Colors Bible in their own language to help them follow Jesus Christ.

If you would like to help children learn to trust God and walk with Him through The Shapes & Colors Bible, please send your tax deductible gift to:

The Smart Life Ministries
1649 Springhill St.
Chillicothe, MO 64601